GOOD AS GOLD

BEING A
NEW ZEALANDER

Selected by

John Daley

GODWIT

National Library of New Zealand Cataloguing-in-Publication Data

Good as gold : being a New Zealander / selected by John Daley.
ISBN 1-86962-098-4
1. New Zealand—Quotations, maxims, etc. 2. Quotations, English.
I. Daley, John.
828.02—dc 21

A GODWIT BOOK
published by
Random House New Zealand
18 Poland Road, Glenfield, Auckland, New Zealand
www.randomhouse.co.nz

First published 2002

ISBN 1 86962 098 4

Text and cover design: Inhouse Design / Janet Hunt
Layout: Janet Hunt
Printed in China

To Margie,
Nicholas, Rebecca, Stephanie, Angela and Catriona
'Good as Gold'

ACKNOWLEDGEMENTS

I wish to express my gratitude to the following people who had a part in *Good as Gold*: Kathlene Fogarty who has a quotation for every conceivable occasion. The superb staff of the Auckland Public Library. My late father, James Daley, book-lover and librarian who would have enjoyed every bit of it. Lillian Joyce and the people of the Papakura Marae. Jane Connor of Godwit, with whom I spent pleasant hours sorting and debating and discarding and reinstating hundreds of quotations. Tom Beran who picked up the task of editing from Jane and carried it with equal enthusiasm. And everyone at Random House who make this business such a pleasure.

Most importantly, the people who understand the uniqueness of being a New Zealander, and have the words to paint the pictures.

INTRODUCTION

My dad used to tell a story of New Zealand forces marching in a parade along with troops from the United States. The Americans marched with a banner held aloft which showed their crest and boldly stated 'SECOND TO NONE'. The Kiwis came along behind them holding their own rather freshly painted banner which read 'NONE'.

We do have our own language, our own culture and our own peculiar sense of humour. And we kow-tow to no one.

New Zealanders can go anywhere and do anything, and we like to think 'on the quiet' that we can probably do it better than most, but we don't like anyone getting too flashy about it. The 'stroppy poppy choppers' have thrived here for years and done rather too good a job of keeping us in our place. But as we become more global perhaps we have to remind ourselves occasionally how unique and privileged we really are. It's no secret that per head of population we excel in all sorts of areas, but throw out the population criteria and we're still the safest, greenest, most pleasant place on earth one can imagine.

The scale of New Zealand makes it possible to achieve, to have some recognition. Many of our greatest names have come from the small towns. From small towns we feel we have to prove ourselves in the big cities; from the big cities we prove ourselves to the world. Because it is accessible, we try harder; we believe anything is possible. Working on the great O.E., the rite of passage of young New Zealanders more than any other nation, we are seen trying harder, giving value for money, initiative, innovation and the old 'number 8' mentality of fixing it and just getting on with the job.

New Zealand was possibly the last place on earth to be discovered and we are as far as it is possible to get from the overcrowding and pollution and fear that much of the world lives with. As Fred said, 'We don't know how lucky we are to live in this joint!'

I have travelled to some pretty remote corners of the world and always felt I had a special visa that comes implicit with the New Zealand passport. Given that someone has actually heard of our country, it allows us an entry to places and people and opportunities that others may not get. It's a bit of an exclusive club, being a New Zealander. Yes, we have the language and the culture and that sense of humour, but sometimes you have to be a member of the club to understand it. That doesn't take away from anything — it just makes us that much more unique.

As the poet Allen Curnow, in his guise of Whim Wham, wrote:

> Hooray for You, Hooray for Me,
> Hooray for Us, with huge Ovations!
> Alas for them, Alack for Those
> Who are not We, poor Other Nations!
>
> The ragtag Rest, who are not blest
> Like Us, with Nothing but the Best!

The quotes that follow are part of a diverse and motley collection that may not always appear to hang together, but they all without fail ring bells for me and remind me of the uniqueness and privilege of being a New Zealander. I hope they do it for you.

John Daley

1. *Alexandre Dumas*

Precisely at the antipodes of Paris, lost amid the great southern ocean, there extends, stretching north and south, a land almost as large as France and in shape like Italy, cut at a third of its length by a strait dividing it into two islands.

This is New Zealand . . .

1949 *Captain Marion*; co-author Felix Maynard; translated by F.W. Reed, Caxton Press, Christchurch

2. *Maurice Shadbolt*

New Zealand begins with the sea and ends
with the sea. Understand this and you begin
to comprehend New Zealand and the New
Zealander. The thundering surf is our
frontier. And our only frontier guards, gulls
and migratory birds. With justice, then, the
Polynesian voyagers called the land Tiritiri o te
Moana — the gift of the sea.

1963   *New Zealand: Gift of the Sea*, Whitcombe & Tombs, Christchurch

3. Lewis Carroll

Presently she [Alice] began again. 'I wonder if I shall fall right **through** the earth! How funny it'll seem to come out among the people that walk with their heads downwards! The Antipathies, I think' — she was rather glad there **was** no one listening . . . as it didn't sound at all the right word — 'but I shall have to ask them what the name of the country is, you know. Please Ma'am, is this New Zealand or Australia? . . . perhaps I shall see it written up somewhere.'

1865 Alice's Adventures in Wonderland, Macmillan, London

4. Dan Davin

They got up when it was daylight
and went to bed when it was dark.
They managed the cows
and the cows managed them.

1949   *Roads from Home*, Michael Joseph, London

5. *Gordon Slatter*

New Zealanders
visit at the
back door.
The front door is for
street collectors
and people
looking for somebody.

1959   *A Gun in My Hand*, Pegasus Press, Christchurch

6. *Maureen Graham*

It was love at first sight.
'Marry me,' he said, 'and I will take you
to the ends of the earth.'
She was a good judge of character, so she did.
They went to live in Invercargill and
lived happily ever after.
He kept his word.
She knew he would.

1997   *'Top of the Morning' Book of Incredibly Short Stories;*
ed. Brian Edwards, Tandem Press, Auckland

☞. *Cecil Burgess*

When I came back from the War I landed in Auckland. An uncle of mine came down to meet me and took me to his home and left me with a couple of aunts. One of the aunts touched the single pip of the Second Lieutenant's rank on my sleeve and said, 'What did you get that for?' I didn't get time to answer. The other aunt said, 'Kate, you're not to ask questions, you're not supposed to ask questions.'

I went home to a father, mother, and four sisters and no one ever asked me what it was like. For seventy years no one ever asked me what it was like.

c.1990s

Katherine Mansfield

And from the bush there came the sound of little streams flowing, quickly, lightly, slipping between the smooth stones, gushing into ferny basins and out again; and there was the splashing of the big drops on large leaves, and something else — what was it? — a faint stirring and shaking, the snapping of a twig and then such silence that it seemed someone was listening.

1922 'At the Bay', *The Garden Party and Other Stories*, Constable, London

Lord Rutherford wasn't good enough
to be an All Black so the only future
for him was to go overseas and
split the atom.

1972 *The Half-gallon Quarter-acre Pavlova Paradise,*
Whitcombe & Tombs, Christchurch

10. Rex Fairburn

I have an increasing conviction that I shan't be able to stay away from New Zealand indefinitely... Men are not free. They are bound by fate to certain things, and lose their soul in escaping... This natural scene, in England, is lovely... but I have no sympathy with it... I had rather be beside a smelly New Zealand tidal creek.

1932 | Letter to R.A.K. Mason, 24 June

Down at the corner dairy
the Sunday morning sun
is yellow as a pancake
frying on the sky;
last night's litter
shuffles about in a gutter
and the seedy little shop
stands up and wipes its chin
ready for the day's
business to begin.

It's all old codgers at first,
forgot the milk, out of fags,
wanting, in all cynicism,
the Sunday papers, not liking
the girlies but liking less
to miss them, scratching old itches,
lingering, fidgeting . . .
Then the kids, shoved out
of tousled kitchens for bread
baked beans spaghetti, pinching
the change for a coke, grinning

all over, playing games, loving it,
sure, little sods, of their indestructible
Sunday selves.

Later the marvellous girls
shiny and slow dressed in sex
full enough to spill
of last night's loving,
on their lips the sly taste of the morning —
and the boys, off-hand and matey,
eyes on the weather, ready
to roll up the day, stow in
the boot, nothing doing
around here, get what's left
of Saturday's grog, bugger off
leave boredom behind.

And they go – cars hot,
sliding past polished like buns
straight out of summer's oven;
where is it, the sun-drumming
dazzle they're after? Who knows —
not us – it's anywhere but here.

1975   'Sunday Morning', *In Middle Air,* Pegasus Press, Christchurch

12. *Frank Sargeson*

But one of my brothers found out a good way of warming his feet up. He stuck them into a cow-pat that had just been dropped, and he said it made his feet feel bosker and warm. So we all stuck our feet into cow-pats, and after walking over the frost it was bosker and warm sure enough. Mother wasn't too shook on our doing it at first, but afterwards she didn't mind. So on cold mornings we'd watch out, and whenever a cow dropped a nice big pat we'd race for it, and the one who got there first wouldn't let the others put their feet in.

1937   'Cow Pats', *The Stories of Frank Sargeson*, Penguin, Auckland, 1982

13. *Linesman to referee*

'You'd better count the players.
I think Meads might have eaten one.'

14. Oral tradition

Listen all men, the house of New Zealand is one: the rafters on one side are the Pakehas, those on the other the Maori, the ridge pole on which both rest is God. Let therefore the house be one. This is all.

15. Princess Herangi Te Puea

The land is our mother and father.

It is the loving parent who nourishes us,

sustains us . . .

   When we die

   it folds us in its arms.

1939   Quoted by Michael King, *Te Puea*, Hodder & Stoughton, Auckland, 1977

16. *Mustapha Kemal Ataturk*

Those heroes that shed their blood and lost their
lives [at Gallipoli] . . .
You are now lying in the soil of a friendly
country. Therefore rest in peace. There is no
difference to us between the Johnnies and the
Mehmets where they lie, side by side here in this
country of ours . . .
You, the mothers, who sent their sons
from far away countries, wipe away your tears;
your sons are now lying in our bosom and are
in peace. And having lost their lives on this land
they have become our sons as well.

1934 | President of Turkey, 1923–38

17. Bruce Mason

The beach is fringed with pohutukawa trees, single and stunted in the gardens, spreading and noble on the cliffs, and in the empty spaces by the foreshore. Tiny red coronets prick through the grey-green leaves. Bark, flower and leaf seem overlaid by smoke. The red is of a dying fire at dusk, the green faded and drab. Pain and age are in these gnarled forms, in bare roots, clutching at the earth, knotting on the cliff-face, in tortured branches, dark against the washed sky.

1962 The End of the Golden Weather, Price Milburn, Wellington

18. Greg McGee

There were times of closeness, father
and son, brother and weary brother, waking
very early on cold mornings,
huddling together under a blanket
in front of a wireless waiting for it . . .
wait for it, wait for it!
— and for a whole generation god was only
twice as high as the posts.

1981   *Foreskin's Lament*, Victoria University Press, Wellington

19. John A. Lee

ON WORLD WAR I:

The New Zealanders were a rough mob. We were going out at the line and marching past a Tommy camp. An officer came out to salute us. He was obviously a gallant officer. He had medals including a VC. Then the silly bugger put a monocle in his eye to salute us. The boys yelled out:

> 'Yah, you silly bugger, why don't you get
> another one
> and stick it up your arse
> and turn yourself into a periscope.'

1978   In an interview with A.J. Brunt

20. *Ben Couch*

I come from a country electorate where life is not too complicated. Back there, when we see an animal that looks like a sheep, smells like a sheep, grows wool, and is not too bright, we decide it probably is a sheep.

1977   Member for Wairarapa. *New Zealand Parliamentary Debates*

The New Zealand terrain is one of lively lumps and bumps, blue jags of mountain, green scoops of valley. The sky is mischievous. Storms tumble off the ocean, loosing rain as hard and bright as rice. Curvy clouds bob so low that if one stood on tip-toe, they might be lickable. The wind has a wicked streak. And the gnarly island trees? They have faces. In the violent gloaming, you can hear them plot. Welcome to Middle-earth.

2001 | from American magazine *Entertainment Weekly*
November 16 cover story on film 'The Lord of the Rings'

22. *Oliver Duff*

. . . *cows make more demands on us than sheep — get us out of bed earlier in the morning, compel us to work seven days a week, drag us half the year through mud and darkness, and in a dozen other dumb but divinely inspired ways protect us from sloth.*

1959   *Ourselves Today*, Pegasus Press, Christchurch

23. Sir Noel Coward

WHAKAREWAREWA

Personally I felt that to be able to boil an egg in a puddle outside your front door, although undoubtedly labour-saving, was not really enough compensation for having to live immediately on top of the earth's hidden fires.

1954 | *Future Indefinite*, Heinemann, London

21. Katherine Mansfield

I thank God I was born in
New Zealand. A young country
is a real heritage, though it takes
one time to recognise it.
But New Zealand is in my very bones.
What wouldn't I give to have a look at it!

1928   *The Letters of Katherine Mansfield*, Vol. 2, Constable, London

Then followed the dimly lit, meat-pie journey to Auckland,
in a shelf-like top bunk when she had especially asked for a
bottom bunk, but no one cared or explained or apologized.
Breath soot-high; voices when the train stopped, voices sharp
and clear as footsteps walking the platform of the station; steam
clouding like cottonwool; heavy-eyed sleep, eyelids sealed
with specks of soot. Then early morning, cold clothes with too
many arm and feet holes, a fawn railway-coloured, blanket-
coloured biscuit; tea; a newspaper. And then, at the end of the
jolting, heaving journey over railway lines that had surely been
cut on the bias, a slow, measured halting, and in the scatter
of people waiting, promising cars and warm homes, crying
welcome from Auckland Station . . .

1967   A State of Siege, Pegasus Press, Christchurch

26. Ngaio Marsh

GLUG, GLUG

Sir, — The standard of radio drama in New Zealand is high and, by the large, it remains consistently so. Why, then, is it necessary, when a character is required to drink, for him to pant, grunt, smack his lips, sigh, inhale like a grampus and exhale like a steam-locomotive? We already know he is drinking. We have heard corks pop, glasses clink, people say 'ah' from the stomach and liquor gurgle. The dullest among us is fully informed. Why then must the actor, too, gurgle ad nauseum? Pray, Sir, let there be less of this glottal insistence.

1967   Letter to the *Listener* September 29; *The Listener Bedside Book*, Wilson & Horton Publishers, Auckland, 1977

27. *American tourist*

I don't care
what anyone says,
those 'Incredibles' are
truly remarkable.

28. John Clarke

[While on 'OE' in London in the early 1970s] I lasted three days [working] at Harrods, but my Australian friend lacked my persistence and was impeached on the second afternoon for putting a famous sign on the main stairs. It was made of corrugated cardboard and said:

HARRODS, NO FARTING.

It was at this point that I recognised the shared perspective of Australia and New Zealand on matters of international significance.

1989   *A Complete Dagg*, Allen & Unwin, Sydney

29. Christchurch housewife

'This is one of the happiest moments of my life,' said Mrs Thomas, of Woolston, Christchurch, when she was proclaimed the 'Champion Apple Pie Maker of New Zealand.'

'Everybody has been so good to us,' she continued, 'and while I am speaking over the air I would like to say "Cheerio" to my mother in Lyttelton, to my friends in Christchurch, and to my husband who is in the audience!'

Excitement was high in the Assembly Hall of the Centennial Exhibition on April 26, when the final of the ZB National Apple Pie Contest was decided.

The Hall was packed to capacity, thousands were turned away, and many pressed round the doors of the Hall, watching what they could see of the proceedings through the glass panels. The four contestants . . . competed on the stage in full view of the audience.

. . . The baking began at 7.30. Each cook was neatly attired in a white overall and cooked at a little table in front of the stage. Cheers rang out as the pies went into the oven, and again when they came out.

. . . A concert was arranged which kept the audience entertained while the pies were baking. Reginald Morgan of 2ZB was responsible for a very bright programme. It began with the Lyall

Bay School Children, forty in number, singing the well-known 'Apple Song', accompanied by Ivan Perrin, the composer.

. . . J. Parker, of the New Zealand Fruitgrowers' Federation, gave an interesting talk on apples, the method of packing apples for export overseas being demonstrated on stage.

At 9.30 the moment for which the large audience had patiently waited, arrived. The pies were taken out of the ovens and 2ZB went on network relay, to broadcast the name of the winner.

A few minutes later Miss A D Rennie, on behalf of the judges, announced that Mrs Thomas was this fortunate person. Miss Rennie explained that it was a wonderfully baked pie, the apples were the correct flavour, the pie was not over-sweet, the pastry was a cross between short and flakey pastry, and was perfectly cooked.

Mrs Thomas disclosed that her husband was sitting in the audience, and he was thereupon called up to the stage to say a few words over the microphone to Christchurch people. Listeners were delighted to hear him say: 'This is the proudest moment of my life, I always knew my wife was a good cook but did not realise she was the champion apple pie maker of New Zealand.' Mr Thomas expressed his gratitude to the Commercial Broadcasting Service, and to all those who had helped to give his wife, and the other contestants, such a jolly time in Wellington.

1940   *The Listener Bedside Book No.3*, Wilson & Horton Publications, Auckland, 1999

These were men. They had taken their choice, sailing out of Galway Bay all those years ago with their few saved sovereigns knotted in their singlets when they slept at night in the crowded steerage, their only assets their strong hands, their endurance, their well-conned memories of the famine and the bailiff they were leaving behind, memories which would drive them and their like to plough a furrow across their future as straight as any furrow on their farms.

1949   *Roads from Home*, Michael Joseph, London

31. *Helen Brown*

Travelling the length of New Zealand promoting my latest book recently, I fell in love with the place all over again. It began in the arrival hall at Auckland airport where I suddenly became aware of the men. A lot of praise has been deservedly heaped on our women achievers, but I had forgotten how remarkable our men are. Could it be that behind every successful woman there isn't just a cat but a very sorted-out guy? Composed and soulful, New Zealand men are at ease with their masculinity. I was reminded of something Joan Collins wrote in *The Spectator* about Russell Crowe, saying he belonged to a tradition of Hollywood stars that has almost died out — blokes like Marlon Brando, in touch with primal manhood. At the same time I thought of Monique, a carnivorous French woman I once knew, who abducted a hunky surfer from Piha. Bustling him off to France never to be seen again, she muttered something about Kiwi men being zee world's best-kept secret.

We have a great deal of disagreeable weather, and a small proportion of bad weather, but in no other part of the world, I believe, does Nature so thoroughly understand how to make a fine day as in New Zealand.

1870   *Station Life in New Zealand*, Vintage, Auckland, 2000

33. *Geoff Cooke*

We know how to beat the All Blacks.
It's just that we haven't found
the players to do it yet.

1993 British rugby team manager; *More Great New Zealand Sports Quotes*
ed. Joseph Romanos, Moa Beckett, Auckland, 1994

34. *Chris Laidlaw*

New Zealanders are inveterate travellers. They know infinitely more about the world than the world knows about them. But New Zealanders don't just travel. They explore; they investigate; they participate; and they cope, no matter what. They can be unearthed in the most unlikely places just getting on with it. If they aren't working they are climbing, tramping, paddling or biking. If it's halfway accessible, there will be a New Zealander there. The spirit of Hillary is everywhere. And, possibly more than any other people on earth, we are welcome visitors because we are open, relaxed and non-judgemental.

1999 *Rights of Passage*, Hodder Moa Beckett, Auckland

Sometimes we went down Symonds Street, but it was much more fun when the tram went straight down Queen Street or Pitt Street, flat out and swinging all over the place, the straps whacking from side to side and people falling on to others as they tried to get to the doors, buzzers being pressed and the rope bell jangling. Trams were almost as much excitement as trains for hissing and odd noises like 'chuggachugga', and lurching around.

We always went to Adams Bruce and got huge ice creams and Mum bought some genoa cake, which she said was the best, even though her genoa cake was good too . . .

Then we had to drag around the dress shops like Milne & Choyce, George Courts and Smith & Caughey, while Mum had tons of bolts of cloth rolled out on the counters, and she felt them and said they weren't as good as they used to be, and then didn't buy anything.

After that we got the free bus to Farmers, which was the first trolley bus. Farmers had Hector the parrot, who was supposed to be 108 years old, but Mum reckoned there had been more than one Hector . . . We always went up on top of Farmers for lunches and rides . . .

We loved walking up Queen Street and looking at all the toys and books, and they took us after lunch to the flicks. We liked the Civic best because it had a huge sky inside and when the lights went out it went from blue to black and stars came out. We saw *Snow White and the Seven Dwarfs*, which wasn't so good because the main person was a girl . . .

1987   *The Kid from Matata, Memories of a Post War Pakeha Childhood,*
Grantham House, Wellington

'Oh, strike, how did you get that
wonderful line of yours in **Sings Harry**:
"And the river running down?" ' I asked
Denis Glover at Onekaka.
'It always moves me, deeply.'

'Where the hell,' replied the poet,
'do you expect a bloody river to run?'

1990 | *Jim Henderson's Home Country*, Grantham House, Wellington

37. *Kenji Inove*

In my youth Japan was defeated. The United States' Red Arrows were stationed here and they were active and outgoing. Some New Zealand soldiers were also stationed in Yamaguchi City. They were more shy and reserved; well-mannered and polite – like Samurai.

So I said to myself, 'New Zealand is a gentleman's country.'

1980 At reception for New Zealand teachers, Yamaguchi City, 25 November. As translated by Mr Yoshida, Japanese Foreign Office

Iwas about 12 at the time, lying very still on a bed in the casualty department of the Palmerston North hospital. Muddy rugby boots protruded from one end of a grey blanket and a bespectacled head from the other. It was late on a winter Saturday afternoon and thin light filtered reluctantly through the screens that separated me from the other rugby wounded and the groaning casualties of our second great national sport, the road toll. Doctors and nurses from time to time loomed up beside me and, after taking my pulse and shining lights in my eyes, inquired gently if I knew why I was there. I smiled bravely and shook my head. For the life of me I couldn't remember – which was silly really as I had been admitted the previous Saturday for exactly the same thing.

When my mother arrived the house surgeon took her to one side and offered her a cup of tea and a wine biscuit. Mum drained the cup in a single sip, dispatched the wine biscuit with similar efficiency and, looking the surgeon straight in the eye, demanded to know the truth, the whole truth, and nothing but the truth.

'Okay,' said the surgeon evenly, 'but I can't guarantee that you will find it pleasant.'

'Well in that case you water it down as you see fit. The half-truth, the whole half-truth and nothing but the half-truth is fine with me.' And she sat down and braced herself for the worst. He placed one hand tenderly on hers and began to explain about the brain being a soft friable organ encased in a rigid bony container, the cranium.

'Like a spongy pud in a bucket,' said Mum helpfully, though close to tears as the full enormity of my injuries dawned on her.

'Up to a point perhaps,' continued the house-surgeon, clearly impressed with her metaphorical skills. 'Anyway your son's cranium does not afford his spongy pud, I beg your pardon, his cerebral cortex, the protection it requires. Hence his two trips here in concussion.'

'Succession surely?' said Mum, triumphantly correcting his English.

He looked at her strangely. 'Concussion two weeks in a row is a very serious matter, Mrs Scott.'

'Fair enough. I'll have a chat to the coach and see if I can get him shifted across from tight-head prop to loose-head.'

'We are talking now about the strong possibility of permanent brain damage,' he said sharply. 'Mrs Scott, if that boy of yours gets kicked in the head once more he could spend the rest of his life painting Christmas cards with a brush strapped to his forehead!'

'He'd love that . . . he does a corker horse's head in pastel without looking at pictures or anything. That and Spanish galleons.'

'Mrs Scott, I'm afraid that you're going to have to come to terms with the fact that your son may never play rugby again.'

'No! No! Please God its not true!' she sobbed.

He put his arms around her shoulders as her body shook with grief, thinking to himself how much he hated this aspect of his job and wondering why they didn't get a young policeman in to do it.

'It's worse than that . . .' he added softly. Wiping her nose on his sleeve, Mum looked up. 'You don't mean . . .'

'Yes. You would have found out sooner or later anyway. Your son will be able to play soccer at high school. . .' His voice trailed off and my mother's screaming reverberated down the corridor. Just when they thought she might swallow her tongue and choke she stopped as suddenly as she had begun, a look of half-mad, wild hope suffusing her puffy face.

'You could put him to sleep right now couldn't you, doctor? I mean no one need ever know . . .'

Why on earth, you might well ask, does THE ECONOMIST devote so much more space to New Zealand, a tiny country of only 3.5m people, than to other nations of similar size, such as Albania or Uruguay?
The answer, quite simply, is that the country merits it.

1996 The Economist Newspaper Limited, London, 19 October

I got a job felling timber for a
joker called Dan Hartshorne.
A great big bloke he was.
Stood a good twenty-four hands.
About four axe-handles across the
shoulders, face on him like a
pine-cone and hard as a
fencer's fingernail . . .

1961   *Hang on a Minute, Mate,* A.H. & A.W. Reed, Wellington

It's only a hundred years since men dressed as chimneys, in top hats and black stove-pipes, women dressed as great bells, tiny feet as clappers, stepped ashore at Te Parenga from a broad-bellied, wind-billowed ship. They brought with them grain and root, tilling and harvest; timber trees, fruit trees, flowers, shrubs, grass; sheep, cows, horses, deer, pigs, rabbits, fish, bees; language, law, custom, clocks and coinage; Queen Victoria and her views on Heaven and Earth; The Trinity; Santa Claus and the imagery of snow where no snow will ever fall at Christmas; a thousand years of history, a shoal of shibboleths, taboos and prohibitions and the memory of a six-months' voyage. They threw them all together in a heap and stepped ashore to slash the bush, banish the natives and pray silently far into the night. They left some of the pohutukawas, and Rangitoto was beyond their reach.

THIS IS TE PARENGA: MY HERITAGE, MY WORLD.

1962   *The End of the Golden Weather*, Price Milburn, Wellington

12. *Maurice Shadbolt*

What is he then, this human kiwi who can climb Everest first, or run the world's fastest mile; who can shear more sheep in a day than any other man in the world; who, offering himself for export, can split the atom or send a rocket to Venus? . . . A man of action then? Yes, but a dreamer too.

1963 *New Zealand: Gift of the Sea*, Whitcombe & Tombs, Christchurch

43. Temple Sutherland

[On migrating from Scotland to New Zealand as a young man] there were all sorts of diverting new experiences to enjoy and interesting new words and useages to master. I found, for instance, that you didn't have to be even mildly dishonest to be 'crook' – only unwell. Also that while recuperating you usually passed through an intermediate state of being 'not too flash' before you went back to being 'near enough' again.

Also there were shades of near enoughness – your own, which meant 'quite satisfactory' or the other fellow's which could be suspect. The best-known illustration of this is probably the story of the fencer who tells his assistant to run his eye along the fence to see that the post he has just sunk is in line. 'She's near enough,' says the assistant, sighting along the fence. 'Near enough's not good enough – its got to be dead right,' the fencer insists. 'But that's what it is,' protests his off-sider. 'She's plumb centre.' 'Oh, well,' says the fencer, mollified, 'she's near enough.'

1956 | *Green Kiwi*, Michael Joseph, London

To keep tiny flies out of safe,
keep a small spider in one corner.
Put a few grains of sugar in every
other day, and he will keep your
safe free of tiny flies in return for
an undisturbed home.

1939   *Aunt Daisy's Book of Handy Hints*, Whitcombe & Tombs, Christchurch

Buckingham Palace in winter can be cold and cheerless and there are times when Her Majesty the Queen stares for days on end down the broad Mall to where Marble Arch looms through the mist and rain.

On one such afternoon the Queen, sitting near the window, is draped in a tartan car rug and the Duke is busy beneath a giant portrait of William of Orange, belting a recalcitrant radiator with his sword.

'Philip?'

'Yes dear?' He is sweating profusely by now and has his sleeves rolled up. Sparks fly with every blow.

'Philip . . . how can I put this . . . Philip, why don't we chuck it all in and buy a pub in Cornwall? I could work for Meals on Wheels in my spare time and you could amuse the customers with your sailing stories.'

He says nothing and she waves at the window. 'If only I could be certain they cared. There are times when I feel so redundant.'

There is a long silence. Finally Philip whispers softly: 'Let's give New Zealand one more try. You always feel better after New Zealand . . .'

1977   'Royal Tour Notebook', *The Listener Bedside Book No 2*, March 26

Through the singing of birds I rise
slowly from sleep; this garden, the city,
these islands have moved into morning;
over the sea that wraps the unreachable
curves of the earth, continents sleep.

1980   'Moning in Christchurch', *Salt from the North: Poems*,
Oxford University Press, Auckland

The United States invented the space shuttle, the atomic bomb and Disneyland. We have 35 times more land than New Zealand, 80 times the poulation, 144 times the gross national product and 220 times as many people in jail.

Many of our big cities have more kilometres of freeway than all of New Zealand, our 10 biggest metropolises each have more people than all of New Zealand, and metropolitan Detroit has more cars on the road than all of New Zealand.

So how come a superpower of 270 million got routed in the America's Cup, the world's most technically oriented yacht race, by a country of 3.5 million that outproduces us only in sheep manure?

Then there was the vicar's piano, which had led to my present predicament. The vicar of Kaikohe had asked me if I could bring his piano from Auckland next time I went as he didn't want to trust it to the tender loving care of the New Zealand Railways. I had been only too happy to oblige, for surely by helping the vicar I would be getting God on my side, and that couldn't do any harm. So the piano had been duly loaded behind six tonnes of beer for the Opononi pub, and on the way through Kaikohe at daylight next morning, I backed down the vicar's driveway to unload the instrument. Nobody told me the driveway was built over the septic tank . . .

It took three hours to extricate the truck. The local traffic cop, who had been trying to nail me for some time over these illegal trips to Auckland, could scarcely believe his good fortune when, driving to work, what should he see but six tonnes of beer on the vicar's front lawn and a large tractor pulling my truck out of the septic tank.

The piano survived the ordeal and the beer was finally delivered to the pub at Opononi, by which time I realised the truck had a broken spring. I was replacing this spring when the truck fell on me. I was beginning to wonder whose side God was on.

I did some thinking, lying there [in hospital] with the Angel waiting on me hand and foot. There were two things I had long wanted to do. One was to sail a boat around the South Seas. The other was to go to Canada, to live. These things were going through my mind as the Angel was giving me a sponge bath, and I suddenly realised there was a third thing I'd like to do — take her with me.

Later, when I told my mother I was going to build a boat and sail to Canada, she said I was crazy. Then I told her I was going to marry a Catholic. That rocked her to her Protestant core. When I said that the Catholic was also Maori, I thought she was going to faint. I might have fainted myself if I'd known I would be sleeping with a direct desendant of Willi Tawhai, the last convicted cannibal in New Zealand.

1994   From Kauri Trees to Sunlit Seas, Godwit, Auckland

DO-IT-YOURSELF VERANDA BLINDS

Blinds for Veranda. — Procure as many 200lb. flour bags as required, and stitch together with a machine. Be sure to make hems for rods to go through. Next get 3 or 4 old red inner tubes from a garage, cut them into small pieces, and put into an old tin or dish with raw linseed oil to cover. Heat very carefully on stove for 2 hours or so, until most of the rubber is melted. Spread out blind on ground, paint one side carefully with the mixture, using a brush. Hang blind on line to dry thoroughly — may take 3 or 4 days. Then paint other side and dry it. All stickiness must disappear. Result — a pretty brick-red blind, waterproof. May be painted with black stripes.

50. *Frank Sheldon Anthony*

The Boons had a herd of thirty cows, and put seven milkers into the shed to milk them. An hour's work and they were done. Before milking, they made a hearty meal of cups of tea and bread and butter and cake. After milking, they made a hearty meal of breakfast, porridge with cream, then ham and eggs. About half past ten in the forenoon, a jug of hot tea and a basket of scones was always taken out into the paddock for Farmer, as a refresher, and at mid-day they had a three-course dinner. Then at four in the afternoon, afternoon tea was served before the evening milking, and at six the family sat down to tea. Then supper at nine o'clock, and they were ready for bed. The whole family from Farmer Dan down to the smallest boy, believed that if they missed one of these feeds, they'd die of starvation.

1920s   *Gus Tomlins*, Auckland University Press, Auckland, 1977

51. *Rosie Scott*

I have learnt during my frequent stays in other places that my attachment to New Zealand and my sense of nationality are, on one level, purely visceral. A glimpse of clean, clear landscape, the purity of light, a Maori waiata, a gust of fresh west coast wind, that special brand of New Zealand gentleness and decency, certain faces, the scent of gorse — all of these offer a short-cut of instant identification, a certainty about belonging that cannot be easily expressed in words.

. . . being a Pakeha New Zealander has to do with the love I have for the country I was born to. Although this word is highly suspect in a context where cheap patriotism can kill, love is what it feels like to me, and this has probably been the best path I have to 'learning the trick of standing upright here'.

1991 'Pakeha New Zealander', *Pakeha: The Quest for Identity in New Zealand*, ed. Michael King, Penguin, Auckland

The sky lightened as we went on . . . into and through the fabled Mackenzie Country . . .

Beyond the wide and darkish plain were mountains, catching the light, that might have been guarding the fields of Paradise. They didn't belong to this world at all. They were outside geography and history, politics and all fiscal arrangements. They had been shaped, coloured, illuminated, by angelic masters. They had peaks of pearl, gold and amethyst, rising above cerulean and sapphire shadows and final recesses of indigo. I ought to have said that the plain was deep as well as wide, so that these were no looming lumps of earth and rock but mountains that seemed far away, marbled and jewelled, iridescent and many coloured, all along the horizon, hiding some other and better world from us. When they finally vanished, it was not the same afternoon but one that was darker and smaller, fit for peevish complaints.

1974   'On the Way to Queenstown', *A Visit to New Zealand*, William Heinemann, London

An Englishman, an Irishman and a Kiwi are facing the guillotine.

The Englishman is first. The blade stops millimetres from his neck and he is reprieved.

The Irishman follows. The blade stops just above his neck. He is reprieved.

It is the Kiwi's turn. His head is on the block.

'Hang on,' he says, squinting up at the blade. 'I think I can see the problem.'

1995 McGill's Dictionary of Kiwi Slang, Catchphrases, Characters and Kiwiosities, David McGill, Silver Owl Press, Wellington

There was huge love in our family. The times I can connect my father with feelings of absolute admiration and undying love are among the most precious recollections of a lifetime. The best of all these moments would be when I was woken from sleep sometimes at four o'clock in the morning to find a cup of hot tea being thrust into my hands.

'Get it down quick,' he would whisper so as not to wake the whole household. 'We'll have a boatload of fish before sparrow-fart.'

We would load the wheelbarrow with lines, bait and anchor. It would still be dark, but we'd set off down Rewhiti Avenue for the beach, with me carrying the oars and him pushing the barrow. In no time we'd be dragging our dinghy across the sand

and soon we'd be off to our favourite spots, sometimes as far out as the old black buoy.

Then just before sunrise, dawn would bleach the skies, and there would be a moment of perfect stillness when there was no breeze, as if all the effort of the world's breathing in and out was going into the strain of pushing the sun over the summit of Rangitoto. Then the blueness would come and a low molten hump of golden light would spread along the horizon and the next thing it would pump up and form into a blinding bubble then suddenly pop into the sky.

These are the moments when everything that was unexpressed between father and son would fall into place and we would share all the love in our hearts without a word being said.

1998 | *Under the Bridge and Over the Moon*, Vintage, Auckland

55. *Davina Whitehouse*

Oh, wonderful New Zealand, land of equal opportunity . . .

A travelling friend had told me, 'You'll love it. But just be prepared for the fact that the roofs are made of corrugated iron and the windows in the department stores show displays of ladies' knickers with elastic at the knee.' So I knew what to expect. Corrugated iron and knickers with elastic.

We strolled up Queen Street and Archie produced one of his treasured books, *A Dictionary of New Zealand Phrases and Slang*. Before we could stop him, he accosted a passer-by. Reading almost as from a Baedeker guide, he asked the man in clear English tones, 'Say, mate, can you tell me where I can get some tucker for the kids?' The boys and I pretended not to know him and industriously studied the knickers in Milne & Choyce's window. Bemused, the Auckland stock-broker type raised his hat to Archie. 'There's a restaurant round the corner,' he replied courteously.

'Bottler,' said Archie triumphantly. 'Bonzer and hurray.'

1999   *Davina: An Acting Life*, Reed, Auckland

56. Ronny Lewis

It's not a bad job. I don't really get a lot of satisfaction out of the work, but I like the money. Yeah, it's good money and the hours, I like the hours, but if we worked to five o'clock every day and were getting fifty dollars less, I wouldn't go near the place. As a labourer, I don't like cleaning up after all the butchers. When they're finished, they just walk off, they don't have to clean up. Us labourers have to scrub things, and generally do all that sort of thing around the place. Mind you, I can't really really moan because I'm one of the youngest there. There's not many young ones. Everyone's pretty good and the bosses are pretty fair – like they're not nasty, they don't pick on no one. Yeah, it's not bad, we have a few laughs.

One day I was dying to go to the toilet and I went upstairs because I was downstairs working on the gut floors, and when I looked in, all the toilet doors were shut and you could see all the gumboots underneath. Well, I thought, there's people in there, you know, so I went back down and waited for about an hour and then went back up, and the same gumboots were still there. So I thought, there's people in there, but, you know, the jokers said to me, 'Oh, they're only having you on, they've put gumboots there and it looks like there's people sitting in the toilets.' So I race up and barge in, and there's a joker sitting there on the toilet and he says to me, 'Get out of here.' You know, I was quite embarrassed. They set me up, just a joke.

Yeah, it's not a bad place to work.

1982 Christchurch abattoir labourer; 'Working Men', Glenn Busch, National Art Gallery, Wellington, 1984

57. *Colin McCahon*

The real Far North of New Zealand is
unlike any other part of the land. I can't talk
about it, I love it too much . . .
It's painful love loving a land,
it takes a long time.

I stood with an old Maori lady on a boat from
Australia once — a terrible rough and wild
passage. We were both on deck to see the Three
Kings — us dripping tears. It's there that the
land starts.

C. 1976   *Necessary Protection: the catalogue of a travelling exhibition of paintings from
Colin McCahon's various series from 1971 to 1976,
Govett-Brewster Art Gallery, New Plymouth, 1977.*

58. **Steve Braunias**

John Clarke, the comedian previously known as Fred Dagg, told me something interesting about the letter Z when I talked to him in Melbourne last year. It was primarily interesting because — really, I know no shame — I had often thought much the same thing myself. He said all New Zealanders abroad look out for a capital Z whenever we read a newspaper or magazine; that we have an instinct for it, almost literally a homing device, on the off chance it might spell New Zealand.

Maybe he was drawing attention to his own habit. I failed to ask. My concentration dawdled off at that point in our interview. I was too busy thinking you don't have to leave the country to keep your eyes peeled for the big Z. I do this at home all the time, with a book, and suspect it's a shared common experience, a kind of collective unconscious specific to these two islands.

Reading is like a dream. The mind is elsewhere, wherever the book takes you. But you wake up whenever the Z zig-zags its way into view; your eyes instantly widen, you feel like the author is tapping you on the shoulder. Your name is being called out. A capital Z — it can only mean one thing. New Zealand.

1999   'Capital of New Zealand', *Listener*, 6 March

AN APOCRYPHAL PUB CONVERSATION
FROM NORTHLAND

'Gee, the beer's crook today.'

'Yeah, I'll be glad when I've had enough.'

1966 Quoted in Turner, G.W., *The English Language in Australia and New Zealand*, Longman, London

60. *Kate Sheppard*

For over fifty years our Empire has been
governed by a woman.
Can the women of New Zealand now govern themselves? . . .
Do not think your single vote does not matter much. The rain
that refreshes the parched ground is made up of
single drops.

1890s Women's Christian Temperance Union member and suffrage campaigner

We were the last place to be discovered, and the first to see the light. This makes us one of the great experimental cultures. We try things first. Whether it's votes for women, the welfare state or the market economy, powered-flight, nuclear physics, anti-nuclearism, biculturism. First-isms. The _New_ in New Zealand is our reason to exist.

As citizens of the last frontier we still want to be pioneers.

Believe it.

Embrace it.

1999   CEO of Saatchi and Saatchi International

62. *Sir Edmund Hillary*

ASKED WHAT HE DID IMMEDIATELY
AFTER REACHING THE TOP OF
MT EVEREST:

Tenzing gave me a hug —
actually, it was rather nice —
and then I went to the side of the hill
and had a bit of a leak.

1993 TV interview, quoted by K Coughlan, *The Evening Post*, 26 May

63. *Helen Wilson*

. . . I have discovered that nobody ever lives in the backblocks. It is always the other fellow whose lot it is to live there. The most isolated will tell you of someone further back who 'really lives in the backblocks', but when you arrive at this further outpost the dwellers will point to a road or a telegraph pole or mention a neighbour that renders the place 'not really the backblocks, you know.'

1950 *My First Eighty Years*, Paul's Book Arcade, Hamilton

. . . Doris gave Malcolm the option:
he had to choose, her or his bullocks.
"Either the bullocks go, or I go."

She'd enough of running the farm on her own
with him away contracting up in the bush.
She told him straight. Malcolm didn't need long,
gave her his little smile a bit to one side,
he (not one for words) said, "You can't
understand, girl. It takes a man quite a while
to put a good team of bullocks together."

c.1988 'How Moaning and Mourning Became Doris Gibbs in 1933', *Auto/Biographies*, Auckland University Press, Auckland, 1992

65. *Gordon Slatter*

. . . a seven course meal
— a pie and six beers.

1959   *A Gun in my Hand*, Pegasus Press, Christchurch

66. *Owen Marshall*

There are other places, aren't there? There's the old place in the North Otago downs, where the pink road of crushed Ngapara gravel is bordered by gorse hedges with clay sods to fill the gaps and the road runs up the small valley like a stream and the shoulders of the downs are ringed with sheep tracks. Useless pines around the farm buildings heap the pig-pen, drill shed and fowl run with brown needles, and on the shattered branches which weep a whitening resin, the cones are fully open in the drought. There are single cabbage trees on the hillsides and rilled, limestone outcrops, grey where the weathered surface is undisturbed, yellow in the overhangs where the sheep pack in to find the shade. The yellow-ginger ground of the drought has only the thistles green. The house, see, has a red tin roof and a dish to suck a little glamour down from the satellites. Yet the letter box at the end of the track has a tin flag which can signal to the rural delivery in the same old way, the magpies squabble in the woolshed pines and in the copper evening skies the gulls fly slowly back to the shore. But you know all that.

1995   *A Many Coated Man*, Longacre Press, Dunedin

67. Lord Rutherford

We haven't the money,
so we've got to think.

1962 Quoted by R.V. Jones, *Bulletin of the Institute of Physics*, 13

68. Dan Davin

To those who, out of principle, refused to fight,
and suffered for it. And to those who fought so
that, among much else, that principle should be
safeguarded.

1986   *The Salamander and the Fire*, Oxford University Press, Auckland

69. *Helen Brown*

From an outsider's perspective, New Zealand seems poised on a creative vortex, where ordinary people are quietly inspired to produce things of unique style and beauty.

I'm not sure why it happens.

Maybe it's to do with the clarity of vision that springs from isolation; a small population and plenty of space enabling people to have a crack at anything; the proximity of the sea and exquisite landscapes; the influence of Polynesian culture.

And I guess a teaspoon of self criticism comes in handy.

Elizabeth: . . . you must agree that with all New Zealand's faults, you wouldn't want to live anywhere else. No other country would be as nice to live in.

Reg: *Shouts.* Oh Elizabeth!! You can't really believe that. The only reason you think that is because of all the news you read in the papers and see on the telly — and they REVEL in showing us other countries' problems . . . It's all designed to make us feel New Zealand is the only country in the world to live in — and now we all believe it. Just as New Zealanders are NICER than other people. Niceness is in our genetic code. Whereas in fact we're as nasty, money-grabbing, prejudiced, violent, alcohol-addicted, hypocritical a race as ever walked this earth.

1978   *Middle-Age Spread*, Price Milburn for Victoria University Press, Wellington

71. *Whim Wham*

Hooray for You, Hooray for Me,

Hooray for Us, with huge Ovations!

Alas for Them, Alack for Those

Who are not We, poor Other Nations!

The ragtag Rest, who are not blest

Like Us, with Nothing but the Best!

1967 (Allen Curnow), *Whim Wham Land*, Blackwood & Janet Paul, Auckland

PLANNING SESSION:

Come in, Walt, and have a seat. Walt, I'm about to create a country and you're my choice to do the design work . . . Let me give you my general idea . . . I've just about decided it's going to be two islands, so that the sea winds will keep the air clear. I mean CLEAR, Walt. I want everything to stand out in sharp outlines and dark shadows . . .

I'm planning to put these islands in the temperate zone and orient them north and south so that the whole range of plants from the sub-tropical to the sub-alpine will grow. This brings me to an important point, Walt. I want you to design me a green country. I'll provide enough rain to keep it green. You'll be giving me wall-to-wall grass, but I want it neat and short. It should cover the ground like fur. Vary the shades of green with firs, poplars and beeches. Every kind of temperate climate flower will flourish. The roses will be as big as cabbages.

I want the countryside to have your signature, Walt — rolling hills, pillowy meadows, rock outcroppings that would make a good site for a castle, dark copses of trees, waterfalls, a landscape where Snow White and her friends could come around the corner and look right in place. Round off all the edges, Walt. I want nothing raw, crude, rough or unfinished. It's going to be a friendly country – no poison ivy, no poisonous snakes, no poisonous anything! And no billboards.

I'll also want some of your romantic forests, full of flowers, ferns and dappled sunlight. I'm planning to have a friendly chirping little bird with a fan tail that will fly along just in front of hikers like Tinkerbell. Yes, you can also put in some sinister, moss covered trees with branches like witches' fingers, but I want them to be romantically sinister.

Have I thought about mountains? Yes, indeed, and I've decided to give you a free hand in the western half of the south island. Snow capped peaks? Of course, Walt, and glaciers, fiords – anything in the mountain line that strikes your fancy, perhaps even a smoking volcano or two.

No, Walt, keep your seat, I'm not quite through. I'm planning on a lot of lakes . . . The light and shades of blue should be crystal clear, Walt, because I want the biggest trout that a fly fisherperson ever dreamed of to be clearly visible . . . No one will be more than ten minutes from a trout stream.

Do you have a clear picture of what I have in mind? Good, get to it. Have I decided on a name for the country? No, not for certain, but I'll probably call it New Zealand.

1990   American diplomat, 'Miscellany', *Hendersonville Times-News*, North Carolina, 24 August; *New Zealand Wit and Wisdom*, ed. Jim Weir, Tandem Press, Auckland, 1998

The bellbird clearing his throat in the wet bush
To sing more sweetly than an evening thrush
His silver notes, each one a poet's word,
And the shining cuckoo that we thought we heard.

1983   'Otago Peninsula', *Windfalls & Other Poems*, The Nag's Head Press, Christchurch

74. *George Bernard Shaw*

When asked by a photographer on the *Rangitane* on Saturday to smile his brightest at the thought of leaving New Zealand, Mr Bernard Shaw remarked, 'If I showed my true feelings I would cry: its the best country I've been in.'

1934   *The Dominion*, 16 April

75. *Alexander Aitken*

AS A PRIVATE IN THE OTAGO BATTALION, WITH HIS
VIOLIN SMUGGLED INTO GALLIPOLI (DECEMBER 1915)

We rationed with a section of Aucklanders living in
roomy dug-outs close by the trench called Grafton Road,
but we bivouacked out in the open in coffin-slots among
the rhododendrons or oleanders. I brought up the
violin, which for weeks had lain in the empty
dug-out of the Australian stretcher bearer, he himself
being by now ill or wounded. Each night we had a muted
concert in the largest dug-out. My E-string had gone
but a resourceful Aucklander unravelled the strands
of a short length of the six-ply field telephone wire, and
these substitutes served until I bought proper strings
in Cairo next April. There was no room for the sweep
of the bow arm, while the *Humoresque*, or anything like
it, was out of key with Gallipoli; but Christmas was near,
and carols with muted *obbligati* were softly intoned.
In its time *The First Nowell* will have been sung in strange
places; this dug-out under Chunuk Bair must have
been one of the strangest.

1915   *Gallipoli to the Somme: Recollections of a New Zealand Infantryman,*
Oxford University Press, London, 1963

SUMMER

Yes, this is it, this is New Zealand – open, and dazed, and you have sand in your hair and sand in your pockets, and every day is like Sunday. The sunsets are shocking pink, outrageous, would you look at that. The air in front of you is wrinkled with heat. Mt Ruapehu is as bald as a coot, Lake Tekapo needs a drink. You are walking on hard, pale clay. There are monarch butterflies, and cicadas, and moths, and flies, mosquitoes, wasps, ants, and visiting aunts.

We are summer islands – the beach, the dust, the light. It suits us. It *makes* us. It's the way we imagine ourselves, and brag about it to the rest of the world. Postcards from Taupo, Nelson, even Greymouth, and 'Wish you were here.' Some of our best literature has suntan lotion on its pages – Sargeson's *That Summer*, Duggan's *Along Rideout Road*, Frame's *The Reservoir*, and if you close your eyes while reading Stead's *All Visitors Ashore* you see orchards and wharves, bare legs and open windows.

It's our time. A national dress is established: we go outdoors wearing the kind of clothes that make us look like hicks. Summer has a New Zealand brand: L&P, Tip-Top, Huttons. We know what to expect. TV plays rubbish. Some bore gets awarded a knighthood. Shell Cup Cricket. Road tolls. Sex, hopefully. The tent, the garden hose.

Optimists will blandly claim it's always good to be alive, but summer most definitely has advantages. Food tastes better. You're insane if you think anything beats sliced cucumber and radishes in a bowl of vinegar with lots of salt at the ready. Even vegetarians stop looking so miserable, although it's true one of the most pitiful sights of the modern age is a vegetarian at a barbecue. Steak. Sausages. Chops. Chooks. Shish kebabs. Burgers. Prawns. Fish. And by all means try barbecued Wattie's fish fingers. Fantastic.

The humble shepherds who
watched their flocks in the
plains of Bethlehem remained
humble. The shepherds who
came to New Zealand
put up fences and climbed over
the top wire into a new world.

1940 'New Zealand Now', *Out of Town*, ed. John Gordon,
Shoal Bay Press, Christchurch, 1999

78. Jan Morris

Nobody had seen such soldiers before. They were truly like men from a new world, or survivors from an older one. Tall, lean, powerful, cocky, their beauty was not merely physical, but sprang from their air of easy freedom. Their discipline was lax by British standards; they made terrible fun of British officers, and regarded the British other ranks with a mixture of pity and affectionate condescension; but they brought to Hamilton's army a loose-limbed authority all their own, as though they were not the subject of events, but their sardonic masters.

1978   *Farewell the Trumpets*, Faber & Faber, London

Christmas Eve: A day as long as a year of penance.
In the kitchen, my mother's face is flushed from the
stove from which, all day, she has drawn forth cakes,
scones, biscuits, mince pies; they stand on the bench
outside, cooling in the shade, platoons of them, four
abreast, marching into the barracks of abundance. My
brother and I hide behind the door until our mother
leaves the room; creep in like conspirators making
the secret sign of their order, fingers crooked: scoop
them into the bowls of icing, chocolate, lemon,
vanilla and feel the cool, sharp flavours sting our
tongues. Caught once, smacked, sent outside; caught
twice, smacked harder, sent to the beach.

My father comes home early, springing without
the weight of the year. A fortnight to go before he

shoulders the next load of days. He changes into
shorts, fills a glass with beer, bubbles with talk. As my
mother passes him, weary, abstracted, he sweeps her
on his knee, nuzzles in her neck. She screams and
smacks him: the kitchen is full of laughter.

The long, long day falls at last along the beach; the
darkening house is wrapped around with mystery.
The moon peers above Rangitoto, drenching the
lawn in a luminous spray, gilding the flax bushes
and the karaka tree stands dark against a drained sky,
every leaf soaked in portent. Everything promises,
everything endows, with no question asked, no down-
payment: only giving, only abundance. The world
prepares to surrender its secret essence.

1962   *The End of the Golden Weather*, Price Milburn, Wellington

80. Fred Hollows

. . . the noise of rain on a tin roof
when you're in bed at night is one
of the most soothing sounds the world
has to offer. Particularly if it's a bit cold
and windy – you can feel the elements,
but you have a great sense of
protection from them.

1991 | *Fred Hollows, An Autobiography*, with Peter Corris;
John Kerr (Pub.) Richmond, Melbourne

81. *Mark Twain*

. . . nothing that goes on wheels can be more comfortable, more satisfactory, than the New Zealand trains. Outside of America there are no cars that are so rationally devised. When you add the constant presence of charming scenery and the nearly constant absence of dust — well, if one is not content then, he ought to get out and walk. That would change his spirit, perhaps? I think so. At the end of an hour you would find him waiting humbly beside the track, and glad to be taken aboard again.

1897 *More Tramps Abroad*, Chatto, London, 1922

82. *Asquith, 1st Earl of Oxford*

[New Zealand] is a laboratory in which
political and social experiments are
every day made for the information
and instruction of the
older countries of the world.

1900   At the Eighty Club, London. *Strangers in Paradise*, eds. J. Eisen and K.J. Smith, Vintage, Auckland, 1991

83. *Timaru farmer*

With the current concern about crime, the local community tut-tutted when a 70-year-old man in Timaru was arrested and charged with propositioning a young lady against her wishes.

This occurred in mid-winter in temperatures below zero. Amongst the adverse mutterings, the local President of Federated Farmers was heard to say, 'Seventy years old. Temperatures below zero. It makes you feel proud to be a New Zealander!'

1987 *Tall Tales from the Top*, SeTo Publishing Limited, Auckland

84. Stu Wilson and Phil Kingsley-Jones

The College Rifles Rugby Club is in Remuera,
a rather posh suburb of Auckland.

I was talking to this well-to-do lady there one
night and asked her, 'What are the rates like
in Remuera?' and she replied,
'Oh, we don't have rates, only a few mice.'

Anyway, there was a fire at the College Rifles
club and they had terrible trouble getting the
fire brigade because Remuera is so posh that the
brigade is ex-directory. When you ring them
they ask, 'And who recommended us?'

1997 *There's No Rucking Business Like Rugby*, Hodder Moa Beckett, Auckland

It is New Zealand's role to send out its bright young men and women to help run the rest of the world. And they go, not hating the country of their birth, but loving it. From this loving base they make their mark on the world.

1930s   American anthropologist, speaking to Jules Older, *The Listener*

86. Benjamin Wells

Such will be our humble house in the New Zealand forest, and, whilst sitting around our fire on a wet, windy night, with our little ones around us, hearing us recite tales of a far off land called England — the land from whence come the great ships seen occasionally in the roadstead with freights of letters, clothes, blankets and tools — with a pig in the sty, a cow in the field, wheat in the barn, potatoes in the garden, mead in the cellar, honey in the comb, a loaf in the oven, a ham in the chimney, a side of bacon on the rack, and the grace of God in our hearts, who shall dare to say we shall not be happy then — so happy that Victoria might envy us.

1854 A letter from Taranaki to his mother in England, in A. and L. Drummond, *At Home in New Zealand*, Blackwood & Janet Paul, Auckland, 1967

87. Witi Ihimaera

At Te Reinga, at the northernmost point of Aotearoa, there is a Pohutukawa tree which grows on a promontory jutting into the sea. The promontory is called Rerengawairua. Dad, he will be there soon, for all Maori dead make their last journey to that place and wait for the sun to set. He will descend Akakitereinga, the Root to the Underworld, to a rocky platform on the edge of the sea.

And suddenly, a deep hole will appear, fringed with floating seaweed. The way across the sea. A shadow will leap . . . The waves will flow in. The seaweed will sweep over the hole. The platform where he was standing will be empty . . .

1973 Tangi, Heinemann, London

88. John Sherwood

He frowned angrily. '*You talk like a pommy.*'

'*I am a pommy.*'

Bazzer clapped his hands hysterically. 'Hell's bells and buggy wheels, a real pommy princess from the darling old cobwebby Yuke Kay. How long have you been in godzone?'

'*Godzone. Is that a Maori expression?*'

'*Godzone country, princess, is our proud name for complacent, fascist-governed New bloody Zealand.*'

'*I shouldn't get too depressed about it, Bazzer. It's no worse than anywhere else I know, and the scenery's much better.*'

1985   *A Botanist at Bay*, Gollancz, London

ANZAC:

In New Zealand a New Zealand soldier.

In Australia an Australian soldier.

In Britain an enzyme soap powder which is slightly less of a biological miracle than the other two.

1972   *The Half-gallon Quarter-acre Pavlova Paradise*, Whitcombe & Tombs, Christchurch

90. *Lord Bernard Freyberg*

His [Freyberg's] own rugged sense of
independence and dry humour reflected that
of the men he commanded. On one occasion a
senior British general visited the New Zealand
Division. At lunch, he remarked with wry
amusement, 'Your people don't salute very
much, do they?'

'You should try waving to them,'
replied Freyberg.
'They always wave back.'

1957 F. Majdalany, *Cassino, Portrait of a Battle*, Longmans Green, London

To do something well is so
worthwhile that to die trying
to do it better cannot be foolhardy.
It would be a waste of life to do
nothing with one's ability,
for I feel that life is measured
in achievement,
not in years alone.

1964 | Racing driver, designer and engineer, 30 August 1937 – 2 June 1970

Don't talk to me about the birth of a nation
at Gallipoli or the crucible of valour
at the Somme.
Talk instead of what might have been
without Gallipoli, without the trenches.
Talk instead of the knee-capping of a nation.

1995 *My Side of the River*, Godwit, Auckland

93. Ron Palenski

Spike Milligan . . . once wrote for the *Guardian* in Britain of his love for the game. He explained how he was very anxious to see the All Blacks play Ireland at Lansdowne Road but could not get a ticket.

. . . I went over to Dublin because I knew there were bound to be touts outside the ground. So I went around saying, 'Anybody got a ticket? Anybody got a ticket?'

This woman came over to me and said, 'Yes, I've got a ticket.' I said, 'Well, how much?' And she said: 'Two hundred pounds.' I said: 'Two hundred pounds? For that sort of money I could get the most beautiful woman in Dublin.' To which she replied: 'Ah, yes, but she certainly would not give you 45 minutes each way with a wonderful brass band playing in the middle.'

2001   *The Jersey, The Pride and the Passion, the Guts and the Glory: What it Means to Wear an All Black Jersey*, Hodder Moa Beckett, Auckland

94. Sir A.P. Herbert

New Zealand is a darling. She is more English than the English, more loyal than the Crown; she is as small as Great Britain and as hospitable as the United States; she has a population of a million odd and she produces more per head (including newspapers) than any country in the world; ninety-eight percent of her is pure British stock, which is more than can be said of Britain; and there can be no other place where the English tongue is by every class so purely spoken and with so little of accent, dialect or twang. She is beautiful and prosperous and democratic and conservative; she has every virtue and every charm. But why, I wonder, in a country so full of pleasant things, are they so proud of Rotorua?

1925   Writer for *Punch* and former British MP. *Strangers in Paradise*, eds. J. Eisen and K.J. Smith, Vintage, Auckland, 1991

95. *Rupert Brooke*

New Zealand turns out to be in the midst
of summer, and almost exactly like England.
I eat strawberries, large garden strawberries,
every day; and it's the middle of December!
It feels curiously unnatural, perverse, like some
frightful vice out of Havelock Ellis.
I blush and eat secretively . . .

c. 1913   Letters during Brooke's visit to New Zealand 1913–1914. *Strangers in Paradise*, eds. J. Eisen and K.J. Smith, Vintage, Auckland, 1991

So if I had to answer the question how did Russell and I know we were loved, I would look backwards over my right shoulder and see an immense trail, like an army disappearing over a continent of time: a queue of meals, cakes, biscuits, puddings, bottles of preserved fruits, entire Christmas cakes delivered in their tins, plates of cheese busters hot and crisp from the oven, pikelets bubbling on a greased element, brandy snaps rolled around the handle of a wooden spoon. And if I had to balance the difficulties my mother had in coming to terms with the fact she had two sons who were homosexual — how she struggled with this, tried to make us reject our own native sexuality, then finally came to terms with it — I would place in the scales the never-ending trail into the past. This is how we knew we were loved in the end — we were nourished.

2001 | *Long Loop Home*, Vintage, Auckland

97. John McLachlan

I am a colonist, and so was my wife. We have twelve children, who, as they were born in New Zealand, are not colonists. A colonist is someone who comes to the country from some other country. Why, Sir, not one of my fifty-four grandchildren is a colonist. As they are not colonists, I think a change in the designation of the colony would be acceptable. Let us call ourselves New Zealanders, and drop the colonial business altogether.

1907 Member for Ashburton, *New Zealand Parliamentary Debates*

98. *Bruce Stewart*

There was layer upon layer of ruggedness. Patches of wet rock glittering in the sun. Far below rivers winked their way to a green lake. Fuzziness hung low over the towns. From my high place I could see it all. I was above everything. All those wild horses. I'd conquered them. No wonder the skylark said I was doing right and told me to keep going. Of everything I could see, I was the highest. I looked down at my naked body. I wasn't a fat puppy any more. I had a body like a man. I'd conquered Maori. Me, Boy, I'd done it. I raised both arms above my head, hands stretched right out and bellowed as loud as I could, I'm king, I'm king, I'm king, I'm king. It echoed back off all the rock faces. All those wild mountains shouted back at me, king, king, king, king, king, king, king.

I tried again in my new deep voice, but it didn't echo as much so I changed back to my high voice.

Look at me Mum . . . Mum . . . Mum . . . Mum.

Look how high . . . high . . . high . . . high.

I'm king, Mum . . . king . . . king . . . king.

Look at my new body . . . new body . . . new body . . .

I stayed there raving, letting my hands slide right over my slimness to my toes and back again. Listening to the deep, far away quiet, and the close quiet. Night covered me. A warm blanket. I lay on the earth. I stayed all night on top of Maori.

c. 1982   'Papa', *Lake, Mountain, Tree*, Godwit, Auckland, 1998

. . . not all the fifty-two participating nations greeted the Führer with respect.

When the New Zealand contingent appeared, led by Lovelock carrying the flag, it followed Mexico and Monaco. Removing the straw boaters they wore and clasping them to their chests, the seven Kiwis saluted a lone SA trooper with a zipper moustache who was standing on a pedestal beside the track some fifty metres before Hitler's box. By the time they had drawn abreast of Hitler, the New Zealanders, taking their cue from Lovelock in front, had put on their boaters and were staring straight ahead. New Zealand saluted the wrong man.

1992 'The Man from Nowhere', Into the Field of Play, ed. Lloyd Jones, Tandem Press, Auckland

Many older readers will recall an earlier time in New Zealand, a vivid and exhilarating time when a young nation, poised on the threshold of greatness, called forth from its ranks a natural leader.

From the starkly beautiful central North Island, erosion capital of the world and home of the Raurimu Spiral, came a figure uniquely attuned to the hour. No problem was too great, no matter so Byzantine in its complexity that he could not cut to its heart. He was fair-minded in all things, graceful under pressure and was capable of developing strong opinions unspoilt by knowledge or formal logic. He specialised in the common sense solution and the self-evident truth, and his language was that of Arnold, of Herbert and of Trevor.

His name was Frederick, of the House of Dagg. Born many years earlier, for reasons which need not trouble us here, he had undergone a comprehensive training in all aspects of farmwork and had then attended school from the age of five. His schooling was typical of its time and extremely effective in every way. The New Zealand Education Department had set rigorous standards. Fred learnt that the angles outside parallel lines were equal to the opposite ones inside the lines. He learnt the French for 'big absorbent bath towel'. By the age of 17 he knew the valency of carbon and the German for 'I have fallen in love with the exit to the static air-display.' These skills have not been required nearly as often as the Department led him to believe but there is still time and, should the need ever arise, Fred and a whole generation of New Zealanders will be able to calculate the compound interest on the square root of x, or the use of irony by Jane Austen, whichever is the lesser, and discuss its impact on the Chartist movement. (30 marks)

1996   *A Dagg at my Table*, Hodder Moa Beckett, Auckland

I wake up this morning remembering my past
Those days they sure they sure went fast
Summer days and making hay
It feels like calf club day . . .

And I see my calf, she's got big brown eyes
She's my best friend and I'm only five
And I love it when I feel this way
It feels like calf club day . . .

1994   'Calf Club Day', on the album *Two Timing*

We don't know how lucky we are . . .

So when things are looking really bad
And you're thinking of giving it away
Remember New Zealand's a cracker
And I reckon, come what may
If things get appallingly bad
And we're all under constant attack
Remember we want to see good clean ball
and for God's sake feed your backs . . .

1975   (John Clarke) 'How You Doing?', *A Selection of New Zealand Comic and Satiric Verse*, ed. Harry Ricketts and Hugh Roberts, Lincoln University Press and Daphne Brasell Associates, 1998

103. *Witi Ihimaera*

The moon brings peace to the land and peace to the people of the land. Rangitane, the Sky Father, ceases his struggle to clasp the Earth Mother, Papatuanuku. His tears diminish, he ceases to sigh. Papatuanuku folds the village and her children into her warmth, the warmth of Mother Earth. No matter if they love her or not, they are still her children and she will love them and protect them until, until . . .

The village sleeps.

Rongopai, the painted meeting house, still holds up the sky.

1974 *Whanau, Heinemann, Auckland*

104. *Sylvia Ashton-Warner*

. . . surrounded by a wilderness of ocean, these islands turn out to be the one place where I would wish to be.

1979 *I Passed This Way*, Knopf, New York

105. Rudyard Kipling

Last, loneliest, loveliest,
exquisite, apart —

1893 'The Song of the Cities' (1893), in *Rudyard Kipling's Verse Inclusive Edition 1885–1932*, 1938